GOD'S TROMBONES

Seven Negro Sermons in Verse

JAMES WELDON JOHNSON

DRAWINGS BY AARON DOUGLAS

LETTERING BY C. B. FALLS

PENGUIN BOOKS

PENGUIN BOOKS
Published by the Penguin Group
Penguin Books USA Inc.,
375 Hudson Street, New York, New York 10014, U.S.A.
Penguin Books Ltd, 27 Wrights Lane, London W8 5TZ, England
Penguin Books Australia Ltd, Ringwood, Victoria, Australia
Penguin Books Canada Ltd, 10 Alcorn Avenue,
Toronto, Ontario, Canada M4V 3B2
Penguin Books (N.Z.) Ltd, 182–190 Wairau Road,
Auckland 10, New Zealand

Penguin Books Ltd, Registered Offices:
Harmondsworth, Middlesex, England

First published in the United States of America by
Viking Penguin, a division of Penguin Books USA Inc., 1927
Published in Viking Compass Edition 1969
Published in Penguin Books 1976
Re-issued in Penguin Books 1990

17   19   20   18   16

LIBRARY OF CONGRESS CATALOGING IN PUBLICATION DATA
Johnson, James Weldon, 1871–1938.
God's Trombones.
Penguin Twentieth-Century Classics.
Reprint of the 1969 ed. published by The Viking Press, New York.
ISBN 0 14 01.8403 1
I. Title.
PS3519.02625G6   1976   811'.5'2   76–48270

Printed in the United States of America
Set in Linotype Caslon

To Arthur B. Spingarn

Grateful acknowledgment is made for the kind permission to reprint the following poems: To *The Freeman* for "The Creation," to *The American Mercury* for "Go Down Death," and to *The Century Magazine* for "The Judgment Day."

Contents

Preface

A good deal has been written on the folk creations of the American Negro: his music, sacred and secular; his plantation tales, and his dances; but that there are folk sermons, as well, is a fact that has passed unnoticed. I remember hearing in my boyhood sermons that were current, sermons that passed with only slight modifications from preacher to preacher and from locality to locality. Such sermons were, "The Valley of Dry Bones," which was based on the vision of the prophet in the 37th chapter of Ezekiel; the "Train Sermon," in which both God and the devil were pictured as running trains, one loaded with saints, that pulled up in heaven, and the other with sinners, that dumped its load in hell; the "Heavenly March," which gave in detail the journey of the faithful from earth, on up through the pearly gates to the great white throne. Then there was a stereotyped sermon which had no definite subject, and which was quite generally preached; it began with the Creation, went on to the fall of man, rambled through the trials and tribulations of the Hebrew Children, came down to the redemption by Christ, and ended with the Judgment Day and a warning and an exhortation to sinners. This was the framework of a sermon that allowed the individual preacher the widest latitude that could be desired for all his arts and powers. There was one Negro sermon that in its day was a classic, and widely known to the public. Thousands of people, white and black, flocked to the church of John Jasper in Richmond, Virginia, to hear him preach his famous sermon proving that the earth is flat and the sun does move. John Jasper's sermon was imitated and adapted by many lesser preachers.

I heard only a few months ago in Harlem an up-to-date version of the "Train Sermon." The preacher styled himself "Son of Thunder" — a sobriquet adopted by many of the old-time preachers — and phrased his subject, "The Black Diamond Express, running between here and hell, making thirteen stops and arriving in hell ahead of time."

The old-time Negro preacher has not yet been given the niche in which he properly belongs. He has been portrayed only as a semi-comic figure. He had, it is true, his comic aspects, but on the whole he was an important figure, and at bottom a vital factor. It was through him that the people of diverse languages and customs who were brought here from diverse parts of Africa and thrown into slavery were given their first sense of unity and solidarity. He was the first shepherd of this bewildered flock. His power for good or ill was very great. It was the old-time preacher who for generations was the mainspring of hope and inspiration for the Negro in America. It was also he who instilled into the Negro the narcotic doctrine epitomized in the Spiritual, "You May Have All Dis World, But Give Me Jesus." This power of the old-time preacher, somewhat lessened and changed in his successors, is still a vital force; in fact, it is still the greatest single influence among the colored people of the United States. The Negro today is, perhaps, the most priest-governed group in the country.

The history of the Negro preacher reaches back to Colonial days. Before the Revolutionary War, when slavery had not yet taken on its more grim and heart-less economic aspects, there were famed black preachers who preached to both whites and blacks. George Liele was preaching to whites and blacks at Augusta, Ga., as far back as 1773, and Andrew Bryan at Savannah a few years later.* The most famous of these earliest preachers was Black Harry, who during the Revolutionary period accompanied Bishop Asbury as a drawing card and preached from the same plat-form with other founders of the Methodist Church. Of him, John Ledman in his *History of the Rise of Methodism in America* says, "The truth was that Harry was a more popular speaker than Mr. Asbury or almost anyone else in his day." In the two or three decades before the Civil War Negro preachers in the North, many of them well-educated and cultured, were courageous spokesmen against slavery and all its evils.

The effect on the Negro of the establishment of separate and independent places of worship can hardly

* See *The History of the Negro Church,* Carter G. Woodson.

be estimated. Some idea of how far this effect reached may be gained by a comparison between the social and religious trends of the Negroes of the Old South and of the Negroes of French Louisiana and the West Indies, where they were within and directly under the Roman Catholic Church and the Church of England. The old-time preacher brought about the establishment of these independent places of worship and thereby provided the first sphere in which race leadership might develop and function. These scattered and often clandestine groups have grown into the strongest and richest organization among colored Americans. Another thought—except for these separate places of worship there never would have been any Spirituals.

The old-time preacher was generally a man far above the average in intelligence; he was, not infrequently, a man of positive genius. The earliest of these preachers must have virtually committed many parts of the Bible to memory through hearing the scriptures read or preached from in the white churches which the slaves attended. They were the first of the slaves to learn to read, and their reading was confined to the Bible, and specifically to the more dramatic passages of the Old Testament. A text served mainly as a starting point and often had no relation to the development of the sermon. Nor would the old-time preacher balk at any text within the lids of the Bible. There is the story of one who after reading a rather cryptic passage took off his spectacles, closed the Bible with a bang and by way of preface said, "Brothers and sisters, this morning — I intend to explain the unexplainable — find out the undefinable — ponder over the imponderable — and unscrew the inscrutable."

⊙　　⊙　　⊙

The old-time Negro preacher of parts was above all an orator, and in good measure an actor. He knew the secret of oratory, that at bottom it is a progression of rhythmic words more than it is anything else. Indeed, I have witnessed congregations moved to ecstasy by the rhythmic intoning of sheer incoherencies. He was a master of all the modes of eloquence. He often possessed a voice that was a marvelous instrument, a voice he could modulate from a sepulchral whisper to a crashing thunder clap. His discourse was generally kept at a high pitch of fervency, but occasionally he dropped into colloquialisms and, less often, into humor. He preached a personal and anthropomorphic God, a sure-enough heaven and a red-hot hell. His imagination was bold and unfettered. He had the power to sweep his hearers before him; and so himself was often swept away. At such times his language was not prose but poetry. It was from memories of such preachers there grew the idea of this book of poems.

⊙　　⊙　　⊙

In a general way, these poems were suggested by the rather vague memories of sermons I heard preached in my childhood; but the immediate stimulus for setting them down came quite definitely at a comparatively recent date. I was speaking on a Sunday in Kansas City, addressing meetings in various colored churches. When I had finished my fourth talk it was after nine o'clock at night, but the committee told me there was still another meeting to address. I demurred, making the quotation about the willingness of the spirit and the weakness of the flesh, for I was dead tired. I also protested the lateness of the hour, but I was informed that for the meeting at this church we were in good time. When we reached the church an "exhorter" was just concluding a dull sermon. After his there were two other short sermons. These sermons proved to be preliminaries, mere curtain-raisers for a famed visiting preacher. At last he arose. He was a dark-brown man, handsome in his gigantic proportions. He appeared to be a bit self-conscious, perhaps impressed by the presence of the "distinguished visitor" on the platform, and started in to preach a formal sermon from a formal text. The congregation sat apathetic and dozing. He sensed that he was losing his audience and his opportunity. Suddenly he closed the Bible, stepped out from behind the pulpit and began to preach. He started intoning the old folk-sermon that begins with the creation of the world and ends with Judgment Day. He was at once a changed man, free, at ease and masterful. The change in the congregation was instantaneous. An electric current ran through the crowd. It was in a moment alive and quivering; and all the while the preacher held it in the palm of his hand. He was wonderful in the way he employed his conscious and unconscious art. He strode the pulpit up and down in what was actually a very rhythmic dance, and he brought into play the full gamut of his wonderful voice, a voice —

what shall I say?—not of an organ or a trumpet, but rather of a trombone,* the instrument possessing above all others the power to express the wide and varied range of emotions encompassed by the human voice— and with greater amplitude. He intoned, he moaned, he pleaded—he blared, he crashed, he thundered. I sat fascinated; and more, I was, perhaps against my will, deeply moved; the emotional effect upon me was irresistible. Before he had finished I took a slip of paper and somewhat surreptitiously jotted down some ideas for the first poem, "The Creation."

⊙   ⊙   ⊙

At first thought, Negro dialect would appear to be the precise medium for these old-time sermons; however, as the reader will see, the poems are not written in dialect. My reason for not using the dialect is double. First, although the dialect is the exact instrument for voicing certain traditional phases of Negro life, it is, and perhaps by that very exactness, a quite limited instrument. Indeed, it is an instrument with but two complete stops, pathos and humor. This limitation is not due to any defect of the dialect as dialect, but to the mould of convention in which Negro dialect in the United States has been set, to the fixing effects of its long association with the Negro only as a happy-go-lucky or a forlorn figure. The Aframerican poet might in time be able to break this mould of convention and write poetry in dialect without feeling that

---

* *Trombone:* A powerful brass instrument of the trumpet family, the only wind instrument possessing a complete chromatic scale enharmonically true, like the human voice or the violin, and hence very valuable in the orchestra.—*Standard Dictionary.*

his first line will put the reader in a frame of mind which demands that the poem be either funny or sad, but I doubt that he will make the effort to do it; he does not consider it worth the while. In fact, practically no poetry is being written in dialect by the colored poets of today. These poets have thrown aside dialect and discarded most of the material and subject matter that went into dialect poetry. The passing of dialect as a medium for Negro poetry will be an actual loss, for in it many beautiful things can be done, and done best; however, in my opinion, *traditional* Negro dialect as a form for Aframerican poets is absolutely dead. The Negro poet in the United States, for poetry which he wishes to give a distinctively racial tone and color, needs now an instrument of greater range than dialect; that is, if he is to do more than sound the small notes of sentimentality. I said something on this point in *The Book of American Negro Poetry,* and because I cannot say it better, I quote: "What the colored poet in the United States needs to do is something like what Synge did for the Irish; he needs to find a form that will express the racial spirit by symbols from within rather than by symbols from without — such as the mere mutilation of English spelling and pronunciation. He needs a form that is freer and larger than dialect, but which will still hold the racial flavor; a form expressing the imagery, the idioms, the peculiar turns of thought and the distinctive humor and pathos, too, of the Negro, but which will also be capable of voicing the deepest and highest emotions and aspirations and allow of the widest range of subjects and the widest scope of treatment." The form of "The Creation," the first poem of this group, was a first experiment by me in this direction.

The second part of my reason for not writing these poems in dialect is the weightier. The old-time Negro preachers, though they actually used dialect in their ordinary intercourse, stepped out from its narrow confines when they preached. They were all saturated with the sublime phraseology of the Hebrew prophets and steeped in the idioms of King James English, so when they preached and warmed to their work they spoke another language, a language far removed from traditional Negro dialect. It was really a fusion of Negro idioms with Bible English; and in this there may have been, after all, some kinship with the innate grandiloquence of their old African tongues. To place in the mouths of the talented old-time Negro preachers a language that is a literary imitation of Mississippi cotton-field dialect is sheer burlesque.

Gross exaggeration of the use of big words by these preachers, in fact by Negroes in general, has been commonly made; the laugh being at the exhibition of ignorance involved. What is the basis of this fondness for big words? Is the predilection due, as is supposed, to ignorance desiring to parade itself as knowledge? Not at all. The old-time Negro preacher loved the sonorous, mouth-filling, ear-filling phrase because it gratified a highly developed sense of sound and rhythm in himself and his hearers.

       ☉   ☉   ☉

I claim no more for these poems than that I have written them after the manner of the primitive sermons. In the writing of them I have, naturally, felt the influence of the Spirituals. There is, of course, no way of recreating the atmosphere — the fervor of the congregation, the amens and hallelujahs, the undertone of singing which was often a soft accompaniment to parts of the sermon; nor the personality of the preacher — his physical magnetism, his gestures and gesticulations, his changes of tempo, his pauses for effect, and, more than all, his tones of voice. These poems would better be intoned than read; especially does this apply to "Listen, Lord," "The Crucifixion," and "The Judgment Day." But the intoning practiced by the old-time preacher is a thing next to impossible to describe; it must be heard, and it is extremely difficult to imitate even when heard. The finest, and perhaps the only demonstration ever given to a New York public, was the intoning of the dream in Ridgely Torrence's *Rider of Dreams* by Opal Cooper of the Negro Players at the Madison Square Theatre in 1917. Those who were fortunate enough to hear him can never, I know, forget the thrill of it. This intoning is always a matter of crescendo and diminuendo in the intensity — a rising and falling between plain speaking and wild chanting. And often a startling effect is gained by breaking off suddenly at the highest point of intensity and dropping into the monotone of ordinary speech.

The tempos of the preacher I have endeavored to indicate by the line arrangement of the poems, and a certain sort of pause that is marked by a quick intaking and an audible expulsion of the breath I have indicated by dashes. There is a decided syncopation of speech — the crowding in of many syllables or the lengthening out of a few to fill one metrical foot, the sensing of which must be left to the reader's ear. The rhythmical stress of this syncopation is partly obtained by a marked silent fraction of a beat; frequently this silent fraction is filled in by a hand clap.

One factor in the creation of atmosphere I have included — the preliminary prayer. The prayer leader was sometimes a woman. It was the prayer leader who directly prepared the way for the sermon, set the scene, as it were. However, a most impressive concomitant of the prayer, the chorus of responses which gave it an antiphonal quality, I have not attempted to set down. These preliminary prayers were often products hardly less remarkable than the sermons.

⊙   ⊙   ⊙

The old-time Negro preacher is rapidly passing. I have here tried sincerely to fix something of him.

New York City, 1927.

Listen Lord
A Prayer

LISTEN, LORD — A PRAYER

O Lord, we come this morning
Knee-bowed and body-bent
Before thy throne of grace.
O Lord — this morning —
Bow our hearts beneath our knees,
And our knees in some lonesome valley.
We come this morning —
Like empty pitchers to a full fountain,
With no merits of our own.
O Lord — open up a window of heaven,
And lean out far over the battlements of glory,
And listen this morning.

Lord, have mercy on proud and dying sinners —
Sinners hanging over the mouth of hell,
Who seem to love their distance well.
Lord — ride by this morning —
Mount your milk-white horse,

And ride-a this morning —
And in your ride, ride by old hell,
Ride by the dingy gates of hell,
And stop poor sinners in their headlong plunge.

And now, O Lord, this man of God,
Who breaks the bread of life this morning —
Shadow him in the hollow of thy hand,
And keep him out of the gunshot of the devil.
Take him, Lord — this morning —
Wash him with hyssop inside and out,
Hang him up and drain him dry of sin.
Pin his ear to the wisdom-post,
And make his words sledge hammers of truth —
Beating on the iron heart of sin.
Lord God, this morning —
Put his eye to the telescope of eternity,
And let him look upon the paper walls of time.
Lord, turpentine his imagination,
Put perpetual motion in his arms,
Fill him full of the dynamite of thy power,
Anoint him all over with the oil of thy salvation,
And set his tongue on fire.

And now, O Lord —
When I've done drunk my last cup of sorrow —
When I've been called everything but a child of God —
When I'm done travelling up the rough side of the
          mountain —
O — Mary's Baby —

When I start down the steep and slippery steps of
    death —
When this old world begins to rock beneath my feet —
Lower me to my dusty grave in peace
To wait for that great gittin' up morning — Amen.

The Creation

THE CREATION

And God stepped out on space,
And he looked around and said:
I'm lonely —
I'll make me a world.

And far as the eye of God could see
Darkness covered everything,
Blacker than a hundred midnights
Down in a cypress swamp.

Then God smiled,
And the light broke,
And the darkness rolled up on one side,
And the light stood shining on the other,
And God said: That's good!

Then God reached out and took the light in his hands,
And God rolled the light around in his hands

Until he made the sun;
And he set that sun a-blazing in the heavens.
And the light that was left from making the sun
God gathered it up in a shining ball
And flung it against the darkness,
Spangling the night with the moon and stars.
Then down between
The darkness and the light
He hurled the world;
And God said: That's good!

Then God himself stepped down —
And the sun was on his right hand,
And the moon was on his left;
The stars were clustered about his head,
And the earth was under his feet.
And God walked, and where he trod
His footsteps hollowed the valleys out
And bulged the mountains up.

Then he stopped and looked and saw
That the earth was hot and barren.
So God stepped over to the edge of the world
And he spat out the seven seas —
He batted his eyes, and the lightnings flashed —
He clapped his hands, and the thunders rolled —
And the waters above the earth came down,
The cooling waters came down.

Then the green grass sprouted,
And the little red flowers blossomed,

The pine tree pointed his finger to the sky,
And the oak spread out his arms,
The lakes cuddled down in the hollows of the ground,
And the rivers ran down to the sea;
And God smiled again,
And the rainbow appeared,
And curled itself around his shoulder.

Then God raised his arm and he waved his hand
Over the sea and over the land,
And he said: Bring forth! Bring forth!
And quicker than God could drop his hand,
Fishes and fowls
And beasts and birds
Swam the rivers and the seas,
Roamed the forests and the woods,
And split the air with their wings.
And God said: That's good!

Then God walked around,
And God looked around
On all that he had made.
He looked at his sun,
And he looked at his moon,
And he looked at his little stars;
He looked on his world
With all its living things,
And God said: I'm lonely still.

Then God sat down —
On the side of a hill where he could think;

By a deep, wide river he sat down;
With his head in his hands,
God thought and thought,
Till he thought: I'll make me a man!

Up from the bed of the river
God scooped the clay;
And by the bank of the river
He kneeled him down;
And there the great God Almighty
Who lit the sun and fixed it in the sky,
Who flung the stars to the most far corner of the night,
Who rounded the earth in the middle of his hand;
This Great God,
Like a mammy bending over her baby,
Kneeled down in the dust
Toiling over a lump of clay
Till he shaped it in his own image;

Then into it he blew the breath of life,
And man became a living soul.
Amen. Amen.

The Prodigal Son

THE PRODIGAL SON

Young man —
Young man —
Your arm's too short to box with God.

But Jesus spake in a parable, and he said:
A certain man had two sons.
Jesus didn't give this man a name,
But his name is God Almighty.
And Jesus didn't call these sons by name,
But ev'ry young man,
Ev'rywhere,
Is one of these two sons.

And the younger son said to his father,
He said: Father, divide up the property,
And give me my portion now.

And the father with tears in his eyes said: Son,
Don't leave your father's house.
But the boy was stubborn in his head,
And haughty in his heart,
And he took his share of his father's goods,
And went into a far-off country.

There comes a time,
There comes a time
When ev'ry young man looks out from his father's
    house,
Longing for that far-off country.

And the young man journeyed on his way,
And he said to himself as he travelled along:
This sure is an easy road,
Nothing like the rough furrows behind my father's
    plow.

Young man —
Young man —
Smooth and easy is the road
That leads to hell and destruction.
Down grade all the way,
The further you travel, the faster you go.
No need to trudge and sweat and toil,
Just slip and slide and slip and slide
Till you bang up against hell's iron gate.

And the younger son kept travelling along,
Till at night-time he came to a city.

And the city was bright in the night-time like day,
The streets all crowded with people,
Brass bands and string bands a-playing,
And ev'rywhere the young man turned
There was singing and laughing and dancing.
And he stopped a passer-by and he said:
Tell me what city is this?
And the passer-by laughed and said: Don't you know?
This is Babylon, Babylon,
That great city of Babylon.
Come on, my friend, and go along with me.
And the young man joined the crowd.

Young man —
Young man —
You're never lonesome in Babylon.
You can always join a crowd in Babylon.
Young man —
Young man —
You can never be alone in Babylon,
Alone with your Jesus in Babylon.
You can never find a place, a lonesome place,
A lonesome place to go down on your knees,
And talk with your God, in Babylon.
You're always in a crowd in Babylon.

And the young man went with his new-found friend,
And bought himself some brand new clothes,
And he spent his days in the drinking dens,
Swallowing the fires of hell.
And he spent his nights in the gambling dens,

Throwing dice with the devil for his soul.
And he met up with the women of Babylon.
Oh, the women of Babylon!
Dressed in yellow and purple and scarlet,
Loaded with rings and earrings and bracelets,
Their lips like a honeycomb dripping with honey,
Perfumed and sweet-smelling like a jasmine flower;
And the jasmine smell of the Babylon women
Got in his nostrils and went to his head,
And he wasted his substance in riotous living,
In the evening, in the black and dark of night,
With the sweet-sinning women of Babylon.
And they stripped him of his money,
And they stripped him of his clothes,
And they left him broke and ragged
In the streets of Babylon.

Then the young man joined another crowd —
The beggars and lepers of Babylon.
And he went to feeding swine,
And he was hungrier than the hogs;
He got down on his belly in the mire and mud
And ate the husks with the hogs.
And not a hog was too low to turn up his nose
At the man in the mire of Babylon.

Then the young man came to himself —
He came to himself and said:
In my father's house are many mansions,
Ev'ry servant in his house has bread to eat,
Ev'ry servant in his house has a place to sleep;
I will arise and go to my father.

And his father saw him afar off,
And he ran up the road to meet him.
He put clean clothes upon his back,
And a golden chain around his neck,
He made a feast and killed the fatted calf,
And invited the neighbors in.

Oh-o-oh, sinner,
When you're mingling with the crowd in Babylon —
Drinking the wine of Babylon —
Running with the women of Babylon —
You forget about God, and you laugh at Death.
Today you've got the strength of a bull in your neck
And the strength of a bear in your arms,
But some o' these days, some o' these days,
You'll have a hand-to-hand struggle with bony Death,
And Death is bound to win.

Young man, come away from Babylon,
That hell-border city of Babylon.
Leave the dancing and gambling of Babylon,
The wine and whiskey of Babylon,
The hot-mouthed women of Babylon;
Fall down on your knees,
And say in your heart:
I will arise and go to my Father.

Go Down Death

A Funeral Sermon

GO DOWN DEATH — A FUNERAL SERMON

Weep not, weep not,
She is not dead;
She's resting in the bosom of Jesus.
Heart-broken husband — weep no more;
Grief-stricken son — weep no more;
Left-lonesome daughter — weep no more;
She's only just gone home.

Day before yesterday morning,
God was looking down from his great, high heaven,
Looking down on all his children,
And his eye fell on Sister Caroline,
Tossing on her bed of pain.
And God's big heart was touched with pity,
With the everlasting pity.

And God sat back on his throne,
And he commanded that tall, bright angel standing at
    his right hand:
Call me Death!
And that tall, bright angel cried in a voice
That broke like a clap of thunder:
Call Death! — Call Death!
And the echo sounded down the streets of heaven
Till it reached away back to that shadowy place,
Where Death waits with his pale, white horses.

And Death heard the summons,
And he leaped on his fastest horse,
Pale as a sheet in the moonlight.
Up the golden street Death galloped,
And the hoofs of his horse struck fire from the gold,
But they didn't make no sound.
Up Death rode to the Great White Throne,
And waited for God's command.

And God said: Go down, Death, go down,
Go down to Savannah, Georgia,
Down in Yamacraw,
And find Sister Caroline.
She's borne the burden and heat of the day,
She's labored long in my vineyard,
And she's tired —
She's weary —
Go down, Death, and bring her to me.

And Death didn't say a word,
But he loosed the reins on his pale, white horse,
And he clamped the spurs to his bloodless sides,
And out and down he rode,
Through heaven's pearly gates,
Past suns and moons and stars;
On Death rode,
And the foam from his horse was like a comet in the
    sky;
On Death rode,
Leaving the lightning's flash behind;
Straight on down he came.

While we were watching round her bed,
She turned her eyes and looked away,
She saw what we couldn't see;
She saw Old Death. She saw Old Death
Coming like a falling star.
But Death didn't frighten Sister Caroline;
He looked to her like a welcome friend.
And she whispered to us: I'm going home,
And she smiled and closed her eyes.

And Death took her up like a baby,
And she lay in his icy arms,
But she didn't feel no chill.
And Death began to ride again —
Up beyond the evening star,
Out beyond the morning star,
Into the glittering light of glory,
On to the Great White Throne.

And there he laid Sister Caroline
On the loving breast of Jesus.

And Jesus took his own hand and wiped away her tears,
And he smoothed the furrows from her face,
And the angels sang a little song,
And Jesus rocked her in his arms,
And kept a-saying: Take your rest,
Take your rest, take your rest.

Weep not — weep not,
She is not dead;
She's resting in the bosom of Jesus.

NOAH BUILT THE ARK

In the cool of the day —
God was walking —
Around in the Garden of Eden.
And except for the beasts, eating in the fields,
And except for the birds, flying through the trees,
The garden looked like it was deserted.
And God called out and said: Adam,
Adam, where art thou?
And Adam, with Eve behind his back,
Came out from where he was hiding.

And God said: Adam,
What hast thou done?
Thou hast eaten of the tree!
And Adam,
With his head hung down,
Blamed it on the woman.

For after God made the first man Adam,
He breathed a sleep upon him;
Then he took out of Adam one of his ribs,
And out of that rib made woman.
And God put the man and woman together
In the beautiful Garden of Eden,
With nothing to do the whole day long
But play all around in the garden.
And God called Adam before him,
And he said to him:
Listen now, Adam,
Of all the fruit in the garden you can eat,
Except of the tree of knowledge;
For the day thou eatest of that tree,
Thou shalt surely die.

Then pretty soon along came Satan.
Old Satan came like a snake in the grass
To try out his tricks on the woman.
I imagine I can see Old Satan now
A-sidling up to the woman.
I imagine the first word Satan said was:
Eve, you're surely good looking.
I imagine he brought her a present, too,—
And, if there was such a thing in those ancient days,
He brought her a looking-glass.

And Eve and Satan got friendly—
Then Eve got to walking on shaky ground;
Don't ever get friendly with Satan.—
And they started to talk about the garden,

And Satan said: Tell me, how do you like
The fruit on the nice, tall, blooming tree
Standing in the middle of the garden?
And Eve said:
That's the forbidden fruit,
Which if we eat we die.

And Satan laughed a devilish little laugh,
And he said to the woman: God's fooling you, Eve;
That's the sweetest fruit in the garden.
I know you can eat that forbidden fruit,
And I know that you will not die.

And Eve looked at the forbidden fruit,
And it was red and ripe and juicy.
And Eve took a taste, and she offered it to Adam,
And Adam wasn't able to refuse;
So he took a bite, and they both sat down
And ate the forbidden fruit.—
Back there, six thousand years ago,
Man first fell by woman —
Lord, and he's doing the same today.

And that's how sin got into this world.
And man, as he multiplied on the earth,
Increased in wickedness and sin.
He went on down from sin to sin,
From wickedness to wickedness,
Murder and lust and violence,
All kinds of fornications,
Till the earth was corrupt and rotten with flesh,
An abomination in God's sight.

And God was angry at the sins of men.
And God got sorry that he ever made man.
And he said: I will destroy him.
I'll bring down judgment on him with a flood.
I'll destroy ev'rything on the face of the earth,
Man, beasts and birds, and creeping things.
And he did —
Ev'rything but the fishes.

But Noah was a just and righteous man.
Noah walked and talked with God.
And, one day, God said to Noah,
He said: Noah, build thee an ark.
Build it out of gopher wood.
Build it good and strong.
Pitch it within and pitch it without.
And build it according to the measurements
That I will give to thee.
Build it for you and all your house,
And to save the seeds of life on earth;
For I'm going to send down a mighty flood
To destroy this wicked world.

And Noah commenced to work on the ark.
And he worked for about one hundred years.
And ev'ry day the crowd came round
To make fun of Old Man Noah.
And they laughed and they said: Tell us, old man,
Where do you expect to sail that boat
Up here amongst the hills?

But Noah kept on a-working.
And ev'ry once in a while Old Noah would stop,
He'd lay down his hammer and lay down his saw,
And take his staff in hand;
And with his long, white beard a-flying in the wind,
And the gospel light a-gleaming from his eye,
Old Noah would preach God's word:

Sinners, oh, sinners,
Repent, for the judgment is at hand.
Sinners, oh, sinners,
Repent, for the time is drawing nigh.
God's wrath is gathering in the sky.
God's a-going to rain down rain on rain.
God's a-going to loosen up the bottom of the deep,
And drown this wicked world.
Sinners, repent while yet there's time
For God to change his mind.

Some smart young fellow said: This old man's
Got water on the brain.
And the crowd all laughed — Lord, but didn't they
laugh;
And they paid no mind to Noah,
But kept on sinning just the same.

One bright and sunny morning,
Not a cloud nowhere to be seen,
God said to Noah: Get in the ark!
And Noah and his folks all got in the ark,
And all the animals, two by two,

A he and a she marched in.
Then God said: Noah, Bar the door!
And Noah barred the door.

And a little black spot begun to spread,
Like a bottle of ink spilling over the sky;
And the thunder rolled like a rumbling drum;
And the lightning jumped from pole to pole;
And it rained down rain, rain, rain,
Great God, but didn't it rain!
For forty days and forty nights
Waters poured down and waters gushed up;
And the dry land turned to sea.
And the old ark-a she begun to ride;
The old ark-a she begun to rock;
Sinners came a-running down to the ark;
Sinners came a-swimming all round the ark;
Sinners pleaded and sinners prayed —
Sinners wept and sinners wailed —
But Noah'd done barred the door.

And the trees and the hills and the mountain tops
Slipped underneath the waters.
And the old ark sailed that lonely sea —
For twelve long months she sailed that sea,
A sea without a shore.

Then the waters begun to settle down,
And the ark touched bottom on the tallest peak
Of old Mount Ararat.
The dove brought Noah the olive leaf,

And Noah when he saw that the grass was green,
Opened up the ark, and they all climbed down,
The folks, and the animals, two by two,
Down from the mount to the valley.
And Noah wept and fell on his face
And hugged and kissed the dry ground.

And then —

God hung out his rainbow cross the sky,
And he said to Noah: That's my sign!
No more will I judge the world by flood —
Next time I'll rain down fire.

The Crucifixion

THE CRUCIFIXION

Jesus, my gentle Jesus,
Walking in the dark of the Garden —
The Garden of Gethsemane,
Saying to the three disciples:
Sorrow is in my soul —
Even unto death;
Tarry ye here a little while,
And watch with me.

Jesus, my burdened Jesus,
Praying in the dark of the Garden —
The Garden of Gethsemane.
Saying: Father,
Oh, Father,
This bitter cup,

This bitter cup,
Let it pass from me.

Jesus, my sorrowing Jesus,
The sweat like drops of blood upon his brow,
Talking with his Father,
While the three disciples slept,
Saying: Father,
Oh, Father,
Not as I will,
Not as I will,
But let thy will be done.

Oh, look at black-hearted Judas —
Sneaking through the dark of the Garden —
Leading his crucifying mob.
Oh, God!
Strike him down!
Why *don't* you strike him down,
Before he plants his traitor's kiss
Upon my Jesus' cheek?

And they take my blameless Jesus,
And they drag him to the Governor,
To the mighty Roman Governor.
Great Pilate seated in his hall,—
Great Pilate on his judgment seat,
Said: In this man I find no fault.
I find no fault in him.
And Pilate washed his hands.

But they cried out, saying:
Crucify him!—
Crucify him!—
Crucify him!—
His blood be on our heads.
And they beat my loving Jesus,
They spit on my precious Jesus;
They dressed him up in a purple robe,
They put a crown of thorns upon his head,
And they pressed it down —
Oh, they pressed it down —
And they mocked my sweet King Jesus.

Up Golgotha's rugged road
I see my Jesus go.
I see him sink beneath the load,
I see my drooping Jesus sink.
And then they laid hold on Simon,
Black Simon, yes, black Simon;
They put the cross on Simon,
And Simon bore the cross.

On Calvary, on Calvary,
They crucified my Jesus.
They nailed him to the cruel tree,
And the hammer!
The hammer!
The hammer!
Rang through Jerusalem's streets.
The hammer!
The hammer!

The hammer!
Rang through Jerusalem's streets.

Jesus, my lamb-like Jesus,
Shivering as the nails go through his hands;
Jesus, my lamb-like Jesus,
Shivering as the nails go through his feet.
Jesus, my darling Jesus,
Groaning as the Roman spear plunged in his side;
Jesus, my darling Jesus,
Groaning as the blood came spurting from his wound.
Oh, look how they done my Jesus.

Mary,
Weeping Mary,
Sees her poor little Jesus on the cross.
Mary,
Weeping Mary,
Sees her sweet, baby Jesus on the cruel cross,
Hanging between two thieves.

And Jesus, my lonesome Jesus,
Called out once more to his Father,
Saying:
My God,
My God,
Why hast thou forsaken me?
And he drooped his head and died.

And the veil of the temple was split in two,
The midday sun refused to shine,

The thunder rumbled and the lightning wrote
An unknown language in the sky.
What a day! Lord, what a day!
When my blessed Jesus died.

Oh, I tremble, yes, I tremble,
It causes me to tremble, tremble,
When I think how Jesus died;
Died on the steeps of Calvary,
How Jesus died for sinners,
Sinners like you and me.

LET MY PEOPLE GO

And God called Moses from the burning bush,
He called in a still, small voice,
And he said: Moses — Moses —
And Moses listened,
And he answered and said:
Lord, here am I.

And the voice in the bush said: Moses,
Draw not nigh, take off your shoes,
For you're standing on holy ground.
And Moses stopped where he stood,
And Moses took off his shoes,
And Moses looked at the burning bush,
And he heard the voice,
But he saw no man.

Then God again spoke to Moses,
And he spoke in a voice of thunder:
I am the Lord God Almighty,
I am the God of thy fathers,
I am the God of Abraham,
Of Isaac and of Jacob.
And Moses hid his face.

And God said to Moses:
I've seen the awful suffering
Of my people down in Egypt.
I've watched their hard oppressors,
Their overseers and drivers;
The groans of my people have filled my ears
And I can't stand it no longer;
So I'm come down to deliver them
Out of the land of Egypt,
And I will bring them out of that land
Into the land of Canaan;
Therefore, Moses, go down,
Go down into Egypt,
And tell Old Pharaoh
To let my people go.

And Moses said: Lord, who am I
To make a speech before Pharaoh?
For, Lord, you know I'm slow of tongue.
But God said: I will be thy mouth and I will be thy
        tongue;
Therefore, Moses, go down,
Go down yonder into Egypt land,

And tell Old Pharaoh
To let my people go.

And Moses with his rod in hand
Went down and said to Pharaoh:
Thus saith the Lord God of Israel,
Let my people go.

And Pharaoh looked at Moses,
He stopped still and looked at Moses;
And he said to Moses: Who is this Lord?
I know all the gods of Egypt,
But I know no God of Israel;
So go back, Moses, and tell your God,
I will not let this people go.

Poor Old Pharaoh,
He knows all the knowledge of Egypt,
Yet never knew —
He never knew
The one and the living God.
Poor Old Pharaoh,
He's got all the power of Egypt,
And he's going to try
To test his strength
With the might of the great Jehovah,
With the might of the Lord God of Hosts,
The Lord mighty in battle.
And God, sitting high up in his heaven,
Laughed at poor Old Pharaoh.

And Pharaoh called the overseers,
And Pharaoh called the drivers,
And he said: Put heavier burdens still
On the backs of the Hebrew Children.
Then the people chode with Moses,
And they cried out: Look here, Moses,
You've been to Pharaoh, but look and see
What Pharaoh's done to us now.
And Moses was troubled in mind.

But God said: Go again, Moses,
You and your brother, Aaron,
And say once more to Pharaoh,
Thus saith the Lord God of the Hebrews,
Let my people go.
And Moses and Aaron with their rods in hand
Worked many signs and wonders.
But Pharaoh called for his magic men,
And they worked wonders, too.
So Pharaohs' heart was hardened,
And he would not,
No, he would not
Let God's people go.

And God rained down plagues on Egypt,
Plagues of frogs and lice and locusts,
Plagues of blood and boils and darkness,
And other plagues besides.
But ev'ry time God moved the plague
Old Pharaoh's heart was hardened,
And he would not,

No, he would not
Let God's people go.
And Moses was troubled in mind.

Then the Lord said: Listen, Moses,
The God of Israel will not be mocked,
Just one more witness of my power
I'll give hard-hearted Pharaoh.
This very night about midnight,
I'll pass over Egypt land,
In my righteous wrath will I pass over,
And smite their first-born dead.

And God that night passed over.
And a cry went up out of Egypt.
And Pharaoh rose in the middle of the night
And he sent in a hurry for Moses;
And he said: Go forth from among my people,
You and all the Hebrew Children;
Take your goods and take your flocks,
And get away from the land of Egypt.

And, right then, Moses led them out,
With all their goods and all their flocks;
And God went on before,
A guiding pillar of cloud by day,
And a pillar of fire by night.
And they journeyed on in the wilderness,
And came down to the Red Sea.

In the morning,
Oh, in the morning,
They missed the Hebrew Children.
Four hundred years,
Four hundred years
They'd held them down in Egypt land.
Held them under the driver's lash,
Working without money and without price.
And it might have been Pharaoh's wife that said:
Pharaoh — look what you've done.
You let those Hebrew Children go,
And who's going to serve us now?
Who's going to make our bricks and mortar?
Who's going to plant and plow our corn?
Who's going to get up in the chill of the morning?
And who's going to work in the blazing sun?
Pharaoh, tell me that!

And Pharaoh called his generals,
And the generals called the captains,
And the captains called the soldiers.
And they hitched up all the chariots,
Six hundred chosen chariots of war,
And twenty-four hundred horses.
And the chariots all were full of men,
With swords and shields
And shiny spears
And battle bows and arrows.
And Pharaoh and his army
Pursued the Hebrew Children
To the edge of the Red Sea.

Now, the Children of Israel, looking back,
Saw Pharaoh's army coming.
And the rumble of the chariots was like a thunder
    storm,
And the whirring of the wheels was like a rushing
    wind,
And the dust from the horses made a cloud that darked
    the day,
And the glittering of the spears was like lightnings in
    the night.

And the Children of Israel all lost faith,
The children of Israel all lost hope;
Deep Red Sea in front of them
And Pharaoh's host behind.
And they mumbled and grumbled among themselves:
Were there no graves in Egypt?
And they wailed aloud to Moses and said:
Slavery in Egypt was better than to come
To die here in this wilderness.

But Moses said:
Stand still! Stand still!
And see the Lord's salvation.
For the Lord God of Israel
Will not forsake his people.
The Lord will break the chariots,
The Lord will break the horsemen,
He'll break great Egypt's sword and shield,
The battle bows and arrows;
This day he'll make proud Pharaoh know
Who is the God of Israel.

And Moses lifted up his rod
Over the Red Sea;
And God with a blast of his nostrils
Blew the waters apart,
And the waves rolled back and stood up in a pile,
And left a path through the middle of the sea
Dry as the sands of the desert.
And the Children of Israel all crossed over
On to the other side.

When Pharaoh saw them crossing dry,
He dashed on in behind them —
Old Pharaoh got about half way cross,
And God unlashed the waters,
And the waves rushed back together,
And Pharaoh and all his army got lost,
And all his host got drownded.
And Moses sang and Miriam danced,
And the people shouted for joy,
And God led the Hebrew Children on
Till they reached the promised land.

Listen!— Listen!
All you sons of Pharaoh.
Who do you think can hold God's people
When the Lord God himself has said,
Let my people go?

THE JUDGMENT DAY

In that great day,
People, in that great day,
God's a-going to rain down fire.
God's a-going to sit in the middle of the air
To judge the quick and the dead.

Early one of these mornings,
God's a-going to call for Gabriel,
That tall, bright angel, Gabriel;
And God's a-going to say to him: Gabriel,
Blow your silver trumpet,
And wake the living nations.

And Gabriel's going to ask him: Lord,
How loud must I blow it?

And God's a-going to tell him: Gabriel,
Blow it calm and easy.
Then putting one foot on the mountain top,
And the other in the middle of the sea,
Gabriel's going to stand and blow his horn,
To wake the living nations.

Then God's a-going to say to him: Gabriel,
Once more blow your silver trumpet,
And wake the nations underground.

And Gabriel's going to ask him: Lord
How loud must I blow it?
And God's a-going to tell him: Gabriel,
Like seven peals of thunder.
Then the tall, bright angel, Gabriel,
Will put one foot on the battlements of heaven
And the other on the steps of hell,
And blow that silver trumpet
Till he shakes old hell's foundations.

And I feel Old Earth a-shuddering —
And I see the graves a-bursting —
And I hear a sound,
A blood-chilling sound.
What sound is that I hear?
It's the clicking together of the dry bones,
Bone to bone — the dry bones.
And I see coming out of the bursting graves,
And marching up from the valley of death,
The army of the dead.

[54]

And the living and the dead in the twinkling of an eye
Are caught up in the middle of the air,
Before God's judgment bar.

Oh-o-oh, sinner,
Where will you stand,
In that great day when God's a-going to rain down fire?
Oh, you gambling man — where will you stand?
You whore-mongering man — where will you stand?
Liars and backsliders — where will you stand,
In that great day when God's a-going to rain down fire?

And God will divide the sheep from the goats,
The one on the right, the other on the left.
And to them on the right God's a-going to say:
Enter into my kingdom.
And those who've come through great tribulations,
And washed their robes in the blood of the Lamb,
They will enter in —
Clothed in spotless white,
With starry crowns upon their heads,
And silver slippers on their feet,
And harps within their hands;—

And two by two they'll walk
Up and down the golden street,
Feasting on the milk and honey
Singing new songs of Zion,
Chattering with the angels
All around the Great White Throne.

And to them on the left God's a-going to say:
Depart from me into everlasting darkness,
Down into the bottomless pit.
And the wicked like lumps of lead will start to fall,
Headlong for seven days and nights they'll fall,
Plumb into the big, black, red-hot mouth of hell,
Belching out fire and brimstone.
And their cries like howling, yelping dogs,
Will go up with the fire and smoke from hell,
But God will stop his ears.

Too late, sinner! Too late!
Good-bye, sinner! Good-bye!
In hell, sinner! In hell!
Beyond the reach of the love of God.

And I hear a voice, crying, crying:
Time shall be no more!
Time shall be no more!
Time shall be no more!
And the sun will go out like a candle in the wind,
The moon will turn to dripping blood,
The stars will fall like cinders,
And the sea will burn like tar;
And the earth shall melt away and be dissolved,
And the sky will roll up like a scroll.
With a wave of his hand God will blot out time,
And start the wheel of eternity.

Sinner, oh, sinner,
Where will you stand
In that great day when God's a-going to rain down fire?